Our Own Teachers:
20 Years on Mount Tam

by Janet Keyes

TOMBO PRESS

Berkeley California

2014

Our Own Teachers:
20 Years on Mount Tam

ISBN 978-0-9914630-0-8

For more information: Tombo Press, Berkeley, California 94707
keyhub@sbcglobal.net

TOMBO PRESS
Berkeley California

Dedication

This book is dedicated to Shanti Soule, cook and teacher extraordinary, who for many years brought to us her skills, her deep practice, and her connection to the elements of earth, air, fire, and water. We miss her.

This book is also dedicated to the women who have served on the Committee over the years:

Leah Antiguas
Gail Bennett
Darlene deManincor
Catherine Eisenberg
Linda Bennett-Gauthier
Elise Gootherts
Laurie Grossman
Carol Hayden

Linda Hein
Jackie Holmes
Elizabeth Little
Holly Oswald
Sarah Puyans
Meira Salman
Catherine Skinner
Jane Tierney

This book is a celebration of twenty years creating a sacred space on Mt. Tam. Great love and affection to Jackie and Sarah for their friendship, love and support. I look back with fondness and satisfaction on our years of working together on this retreat, and greet the women who are willing to carry it forward.

Table of Contents

Preface

    This book is about the birth and life of the Mt. Tam Women's Retreat, a silent meditation retreat held each year since 1993 at Camp Alice Eastwood on Mt. Tamalpais, a beloved landmark and hiking destination in the San Francisco Bay Area.

    I began this book in the fall of 2012, right after our nineteenth retreat, at a time when I was very discouraged about its future. The three of us who had started the retreat were twenty years older, and feeling our age. We had been looking for some women to take over the retreat from us and keep it going. We had just finished the first retreat after Shanti's death earlier that year, and we were trying to adjust to not having her presence and energy. Also, we had held the retreat in a new location, in Tilden Park in the East Bay, where there were redwoods and lots of open space. Though the campsite was in many ways more hospitable than Mt. Tam, and had several features that made our work easier, fewer women had registered because it wasn't what they loved, which was, and is, Mt. Tam.

    As I was sitting one afternoon in the circle, a thought came to me. We were victims of our own success. Over the years, through trial and error, we had perfected the retreat to the point that everything moved seamlessly and appeared effortless. Who would be brave and confident enough to take it on?

    Jackie, Sarah and I were tired and wondering among ourselves about how much longer we could realistically continue to put on this retreat, especially now that Shanti was gone. We knew there were women who valued it and who counted on attending it each year, but they weren't coming forward to help us in the way we needed. We wondered whether we would ever find younger, stronger women to carry the retreat into the future. Each year at the closing circle we asked for help, but we hadn't found the women who could take on the organization and planning required. Year Twenty was coming up; we had said we would stop at twenty if we didn't have anyone to carry it forward. Should we just stop after next year's retreat; could we? Would the retreat end with us?

In that moment the idea of a handbook came to me, a manual of how to put on a silent retreat in nature. Though Jackie and Sarah had done most of the organization and planning for meals over the years, I doubted either of them would write such a book. Wasn't I the writer? This could be my gift to the retreat. I could record what we did, and then anyone who wanted to could follow our process and do it herself. Women on our retreat would have a blueprint for what we did, and the retreat could continue. And we could step back and watch it evolve.

As the idea grew inside me, joy blossomed. Not only would our retreat be able to continue, but women, people, anywhere could organize and plan a camping retreat for themselves. The Dharma could spread in this way we had created, connected to the earth and to each other. I started writing in my head.

At the closing circle, I talked about my idea, which had fleshed out in my mind to include not only how to do it, but also what it was like to be on the retreat. I asked women to send me their memories about the retreat, their journals, poems, and the art they had created.

All that year I wrote away, detailing the registration process, the meals, the arrangement of the kitchen. When I finally had a draft ready, I asked Sarah and Jackie to read it; I wanted their input because I didn't have first hand knowledge of many of the things I wrote about. However, their response was, You got it all right! What they both wished for was more about what it was like to be on the retreat. So I expanded that part, bringing in more of the words and pictures that women had sent me.

That August, our twentieth retreat, I brought the manuscript in a three-ring binder to Mt. Tam. I self-consciously leaned it up against the leg of the altar and mentioned it in the opening circle, saying that my hope for the book was that it would give confidence to some of the women present to step forward to help us. Otherwise, I said, this retreat might be the last one. We were getting too old for all the work; our bodies were not what they had been: Sarah was 79; Janet 69, and Jackie, the youngster, at 64.

As the days on retreat passed, I noticed more and more women reading the manuscript. It was exciting and a little shocking to see women reading it, for we don't really encourage reading on retreat. I could tell that many women were touched by it, and a few even came up and said how much they appreciated it. At the end of the retreat, during the closing circle, many women said it out loud. To a woman, they also said, you can't stop now, this retreat must continue. Many of them said, I want to help, and one woman, Elise, offered to help me publish this book.

Sarah read it the week after the retreat and when she finished, she said, "you know, this is really two books." Elise said the same thing to me the first time we got together. So with a little persuasion, I could agree that, indeed, the section about how it felt to be on the retreat didn't really belong with the details of how to put on a camping retreat. There should be two books.

You are holding the first one in your hand, and the second one, *Dharma Camp*, is in the works. I hope that reading this book about what it's like to be on a silent retreat in nature will inspire you to want to participate in a similar retreat. And for those of you who are adventurous and have the interest and skills, *Dharma Camp* will be a guide to help you plan and organize your own retreat.

Women who have come on our retreat find their practices deepen: without teachers to guide them, their confidence in their own practice grows; and by being outdoors in whatever conditions nature provides, their connection to the earth and to one another becomes more conscious. I hope the opportunity to meditate in nature will continue and grow here on Mt. Tam, and in meditation communities everywhere.

May whatever good that has come from our sitting together under the redwoods be a benefit to you, and to all beings everywhere.

May it be so.

Foreword

By Sarah Puyans

When I did my first Women's Retreat at Spirit Rock Meditation Center some twenty years ago, it wasn't easy. In between "sits" I found myself seeking the solace of the wandering trails, green hillsides. In my childhood, my family lived on five acres with a creek running through it. As a tomboy, I spent whatever time I could exploring the wonder of all that lived or crawled within our property. To my family's chagrin, this included frequent household visits of my beloved woodland friends.

As many do, I came to meditation hoping to find relief from suffering. Early on I sensed the wisdom and profound rewards of a meditation practice; yet, when on retreat, each walking period pulled me outside. At the end of the Women's Retreat at Spirit Rock many years ago, as we stood in circle with a chance to share our retreat experience, I suddenly found myself speaking of a vision... of women sitting in shared silence in nature. Here would be the way to connect two parts of my life that resonated deeply. I asked if others might like this idea, and if so to meet me in the foyer afterwards. In retrospect I was so

lucky! Jackie Holmes and Janet Keyes came forward, both being equally excited about the idea, two wonderful women who have become deep friends, and fortunately, both have remarkable talents to assist on our twenty-year journey.

And the women came. We started with twenty-five, and it grew through the years to a maximum of fifty-five. We had no idea what the response would be or what it would become for each of us. As it unfolded, we began to understand the power of the retreat. Yes, we had flowers, table clothes, delicious food and loving support for each woman. But there was a more profound added dimension. We felt it the first time we sat in circle in silence around the campfire with the stars up above, the silhouettes of the redwoods, the whisper of the wind and the owls calling. We were carrying forward a tradition from ancient times of women sitting in meditation in nature, and it was sacred.

I always speak for a few minutes at the beginning of the retreat before Jackie explains the logistics and Janet sets the intention. It's a time for me to welcome the women into the sacred circle…suggesting this be a time to let their hearts open, feeling the support of the other women and Mother Nature, to let their senses come alive to the wonder and magic around them and with awareness, to follow their inner wisdom thus making the retreat their own personal journey. And, judging by the experiences shared in the closing circle, they have done just that. And so have I.

They speak of a chance to untangle their lives, see things more clearly, heal their grief and enrich their practice. The closing circle includes lots of laughter too as some pretty hilarious things can happen with fifty-five women camping together! And… of course, there are tears. It's all there. We've been our own teachers, we've bonded and we've become a very precious, powerful Sangha.

Recently Jackie, Janet and I reflected on how we had changed over the years and how our relationship has changed also, becoming even more meaningful in the past few years. If there is any way this book may assist others in sharing only a part of what we have experienced for the past twenty years, that is my wish.

Vision and Intention

During the closing circle of the women's retreat in 1992 that Sarah describes in her Forward, she stood and described her idea of a silent retreat outdoors under redwoods and asked if anyone shared her vision. Jackie Holmes and I, strangers to one another and to Sarah, eagerly stepped forward. Fortunately, we each had some related experience: Sarah and her former husband had led fishing expeditions, and one time, when the cook failed to show up, she was drafted. After preparing three meals a day for a week over a campfire, Sarah realized she could do anything. For her part, Jackie had run a restaurant for three years, and was accustomed to cooking three meals a day for large numbers of people. Janet was an avid camper and had sat several long meditation retreats; she believed that many women would want to practice meditation outdoors.

In planning the retreat, our interests, skills, and inclinations led us each in certain directions. We worked together on site logistics. Jackie took on the registration; Jackie and Sarah undertook meal planning and preparation; Sarah spent energy creating a welcoming and nurturing atmosphere; and Janet drafted a lot of the early letters and flyers, the schedule, and undertook the creation of the meditation space. We kept in touch with each other and when problems or quandaries arose, we discussed them and agreed on how to move forward.

We never considered having a teacher lead the retreat. Our teacher at the women's retreat lived in England and came to California only once a year. Also we had no idea if an outdoor retreat would work, or if we'd do it more than once. However after the first year, we realized that we could be, we were, our own teachers, and that on the lap of the mountain surrounded by redwoods, we could hold our own space and practice together in Noble Silence.

We put on the first retreat with only a vague idea of what we were doing, and despite that, it was a great success. Meditating outdoors in silence answered a deep longing in many women, and word of the retreat spread quickly. Shanti Soule became the fourth member of the committee in the second or third year. She'd heard about the retreat and was ready to help even before she attended it. At the time, she was a cook at both Spirit Rock and Commonweal, and a teacher-trainee under Ruth Denison, a revered teacher in our lineage. She brought her experience cooking for retreats, and her recipes that were already sized for large groups. She gave us the confidence to continue growing the size of the retreat.

Many of the twenty or so women who came those first years were enthusiastic and wanted to help put on the next year's retreat. We were going to do it again, weren't we? Each year so many women come forward to help, offer suggestions and pitch in without ceremony; many of them have become indispensable parts of the planning and organization.

Meira, Jane and Catherine E. joined the committee at the end of the first retreat. Shanti came next. Shortly after, sisters Gail and Linda G, their friend Elise, and Holly and Darlene joined. Some years later, Linda H and Elizabeth added new energy to the committee. Last year, energetic Laurie, Carol and Leah have joined us. This year, in answer to our pleas, more women, Aviva, Elise P, Laura Jean, Betsy, Mary Ann and Verna, have stepped forward to help with the work. The committee takes on the hard work at Camp Alice Eastwood entailed in cooking and caring for 55 women. And that's a good thing, since we three couldn't possibly do all that needs to be done.

This has been our shared vision and deep intention: to create a place of silence under the redwoods where women would feel safe, well nourished and held, so that they could meditate and go deeply into themselves.

We also share the belief that we are our own teachers: that each woman has inside herself everything she needs to deepen her own practice and that sitting in nature supports and grounds us to enter the silence within.

Chapter 1: Arrival

Women begin arriving after 2:00 on Friday afternoon, their faces carrying the weight of all that it took for them to get here. As they arrive, Jackie checks them in, signs them up for work meditation jobs, organizes parking for the maximum number of cars, and directs the women to good camping spots.

Through an alchemy of intention and good will, Camp Alice Eastwood is transformed from barren dirt, blacktop, and adolescent redwood trees soaring up about fifty feet, into a forest home for fifty-five women.

Women greet friends from last year, strike up conversations with women they haven't talked to before, and look for ways to help. Everyone talks excitedly. A woman arrives with a trunkful of firewood, and one or two women help her unload. One woman helps another set up an unfamiliar tent. A volunteer sets up the little wooden TV tables in the three bathrooms with soap, hand lotion, and candles for later when it gets dark. Another woman goes around the camp and attaches signs with clothespins to low-hanging redwood branches, signs that say Silent Retreat in Progress, Please be Mindful of your Speech.

Janet and several volunteers spread out the tarps for the meditation area near the campfire pit, finding the best arrangement for fire and forest viewing. They thumbtack up Tibetan prayer flags on the canopy and the split-rail fence above the meditation area. The altar faces the trees, the Buddha and Kwan Yin statues and the pillar candle hold down a colorful cloth. As soon as the tarps are laid down, women bring their rugs, blankets, cushions, pillows, shawls, and chairs to establish their sitting spaces. Once that has been secured, they look for a level spot to pitch their tents.

Most activity, though, centers around the kitchen where Jackie, Shanti, Darlene, and others put away the food and organize the cooking and serving areas. Once the perishable food is stored in coolers and labeled, the evening's cook starts preparation for the Dal soup. Several women pitch in to chop carrots, onions and garlic, and wash and chop the fresh dill and spinach.

Someone else lays out the dark green plastic tablecloths on the tables and adds the accent squares of bright fabric printed with sunflowers. Someone else puts out the tea lights and salt and pepper shakers. Nearby, another woman arranges the big vase of flowers for the altar, and six smaller bouquets, one for each picnic table.

If it's a foggy, cold day, a couple of women start a fire in the firepit.

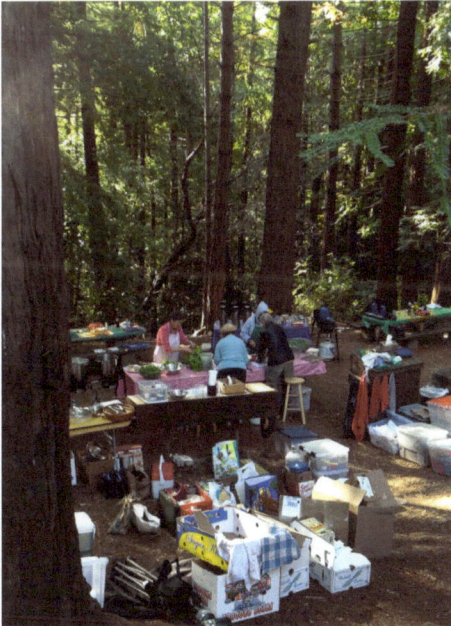

Sautéing onions and garlic mixed with curry, marjoram and cumin, envelop the kitchen and sitting area with their fragrance. The cook adds the onion mixture to the simmering orange lentils, tasting the soup as it cooks for further seasoning. The serving table is set with bread, huge bowls of salad, fruit, and a freshly baked dessert that someone has brought to share.

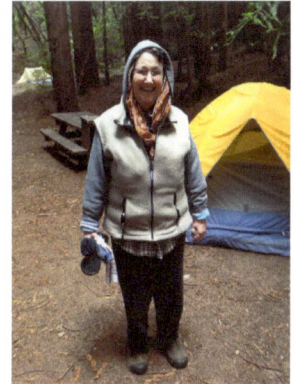

The food is divine--of course. I always love anything someone else prepares for me, but on these weekends, not only do I taste the delicious blend of fresh flavors, but also the caring love, both of which nourish me immensely.　　　　*Nancy H.*

The cook rings the dinner bell, and the women line up with their bowls and plates. We talk and laugh as though there is no tomorrow because this is the only meal where talking takes place. When the meal is finished and the people designated as food finishers are putting leftovers away, the women wash and dry their own dishes and bring them back to their places at the tables. Jackie shows the women washing pots the map of where clean dishes and pots should go. She checks to be sure that nothing that might interest a raccoon is within its reach.

Chapter 2:
Creating a Container of Noble Silence

A bell summons us to the sitting area. It's still light, though the sun has set and the glow from the west is beginning to fade. The fire spits and pops. A few women are meditating already, eyes closed, bodies still; others are wrapping themselves in their shawls and blankets against the cooling air. A few voices are still heard from the kitchen, but the excitement of starting the retreat has mostly gone inward; our anticipation builds. The few women who have never been on a silent retreat may be feeling a little trepidation: How am I not going to talk for two whole days?

I'm kind of a newcomer to the retreat, but I feel like a regular at the same time. My first time was the year of my retirement. I was giddy most of that year, and that retreat was part of the playfulness that came to me with ease at the time.   Nancy B-S

Finally, finished with the last detail needing her attention in the kitchen, Jackie slides into her chair at the edge of the tarp. With all she's done already, you would think she'd be frazzled, but her smile is broad and she takes her time to begin looking around the circle at all of us. She makes some little joke; everyone laughs. And then she begins, welcoming us to the retreat, giving a general overview of the days, and reminding us of the importance of showing up for our work meditation jobs. Without each of us doing our part, the retreat could not happen. She gives us a short orientation about the site, and some general guidelines—please take your shoes off before walking on the tarps; if you need something, look in the plastic bins around the wooden cabinet near the sink. We use the storage cabinet as the Communication Center. This is how we communicate while we're in silence. If you need to tell us something, write it on the pad there. If you're planning a long walk, please leave a note so we don't worry. And then it's Sarah's turn.

Sarah takes a moment to look around the circle at each woman, though individual faces are growing less distinct in the twilight. She tells the now-familiar story of her vision of this

retreat that was born at a women's retreat over 20 years ago, held indoors. She especially thanks Jackie for all the work she has done this year to prepare for this retreat, and she thanks the other committee members for all their efforts. "So much love and devotion go into making this retreat happen," she says, nodding to all of us. And we nod back; we can see how much effort it has taken, and we feel the love and dedication of all women who do the work to make this happen year after year. Sarah says, "I have seen how transformative this retreat has been for so many women over the years and this is what encourages me to continue. Feel the support of the other women around you, the support of the mountain, and the life all around us."

Before we enter the silence, we take a stretch break, just a few moments to adjust our bodies and find a comfortable sitting posture.

Out of the deepening darkness, Janet's voice rises,

"Another year brings us safely back to Mt. Tamalpais. Coming together in community is a precious thing: feeling the many become one, seeing our footprints covered over by another's. Being in silence together allows us to be separate without being alone. In the safety of the silence we discover what we long for, what we need, who we are.

Though this retreat was born during a Buddhist women's retreat, we welcome women of all traditions. Meditation is a different experience for each of us and changes over time as we practice. Whatever meditation or contemplation practice you have is welcome here, as long as you are silent and don't impinge on the quiet of anyone else. Should you get stuck in your practice, and feel the need to talk to someone, find me or one of the other committee members to talk to.

As it has been from our first retreat here, we are our own teachers. Sitting out under the stars on the lap of the mountain, supported by the trees, and all the living beings whose home we share, we feel strength and courage welling gently up from within, nurturing confidence in our practice.

Let us begin now by setting our intention. Ask yourself: Why am I here? What is my deepest intention as I sit? What have I come to investigate or renew? I believe these are the most important questions we can ask ourselves when we begin a retreat, when we begin any important endeavor. The answers to these questions will guide us as we go forward, and can sustain us when difficulties arise, especially as we sit here without a teacher to lead us though the days and nights of practice. So take a few moments now to go inside and ask yourself the question: What is my intention in this precious time here on Mt. Tamalpais?

Sometimes no clear answer comes. Instead you might simply gather your intention to be fully present, to let each moment speak in its own way. Let us not lose one precious moment of these silent days together.

Soon we will be in silence; we will eat, work, and walk in silence. A bell will call us to wake up, to eat, to sit, and to end each sitting.

The final tradition of this retreat is how we hold the container of silence for one another. I would like to invite and encourage you to take a turn ringing the bell that ends each sitting.

Here, next to the altar, is where we keep the bell, a clock, and a copy of the schedule. If you come into the hall and see the bell still here by the altar, perhaps you will decide that it's your turn. Check the schedule to confirm when the sitting ends, and take the bell and striker and the clock, with you to your place. Then begin your sitting. When the forty-five minutes are up, ring the bell.

How will you know when forty-five minutes has elapsed? By looking at the clock. Remember, it doesn't matter how many times you have to look: one, twelve, a hundred; you can check the time mindfully. When it is time, pick up the striker and ring it like this: once, twice, three times. There is a bright state of mind that comes when the bell is sitting beside you. Please take your turn once or many times: Hold the silence for us."

The fact that this has been a leaderless retreat has been great; each woman involved has her own history and education, and it works not to have a central dogma.   Connie

My intention: To be aware of habits of mind and the suffering they can cause. To be kind and loving to myself as I meet each moment.   Janet

My intention is to open my heart, to burn off the worry, quandaries, fear; reveal and open to you, to love, to knowing. Rebecca

Ringing the bell was also moving for me. I feel responsible but not in a difficult way.   Diana

Over the years Shanti, Meira and Elise have taken turns leading the taking of the refuges and precepts, a Buddhist tradition that begins any silent meditation retreat:

We take refuge in the Buddha, recognizing that in this lifetime a human being can awaken. We take refuge in the Dharma, the natural laws of cause and effect. And we take refuge in the Sangha, the community of people who practice together, just as we are.

Precepts are principles of behavior for living together in community; they allow us to be here together in harmony and safety:

- The first precept is not killing, not even the fly walking on our lovely garbage.
- The second, not taking what isn't freely offered. This also means taking only what we need, what will help us in this moment to be fully present.
- Third, not taking intoxicants that may interfere with our mindfulness.
- Fourth, not engaging in sexual activity.
- And fifth, keeping the Noble Silence, respecting the peace of each woman here as she respects and protects ours.

In the many years she was with us, Shanti was particularly drawn to evoking the elements—earth, air, water, fire—which make up this forest, this world of ours. Each of us is also composed of the same four elements: water, our blood and internal fluids; earth, hardness, our bones and cartilage; air, our breath that comes in and out of our bodies; and fire, the heat our bodies create as living beings. These are the most basic elements that make up our experience of living in a body.

Sitting circle

In Retreat
Is the world going away
or am I
absence of words
Big Sky mind with no skywriting
no in and out
no more words
If they arrive they are noted and dismissed
like the sound of
the hammer
the cough
the crow
the crackling fire
and the wind in the trees
                              Djuna

And now we enter the silence together.

At first there are rustling sounds among the women. The air is colder and we snuggle down into our shawls and blankets. Sounds become louder: a few cars wind in and out of the curves and turns above us on Panoramic Highway, the fire pops, distant voices call, or a snatch of music. Slowly the night silence settles around us. Our thoughts dart and flicker, like the firelight, and slowly we feel ourselves coming home to our own inner silence.

Out of the darkness and the quiet, the bell rings three times. We move our stiff bodies and fold our shawls and blankets. Flashlights and headlamps flicker on; someone breaks up the fire and blows out the candle on the altar. The sounds now are quiet footsteps moving towards the bathrooms, the sudden whoosh of water, muffled footsteps moving toward our tents. Later a great horned owl calls out close overhead, and after several seconds a distant response comes from the next ridge. They call back and forth for a long time, until the listener is no longer awake to do the hearing.

Chapter 3: Daily Routine

First light filters through the forest around 4:30, and by 5:00 it's light enough to see the vertical silhouettes of the redwoods. Soon there's a glow coming from the kitchen area—Jackie and Gail have lit the lanterns there, the candles in the meditation area, and the tea lights on the tables. Gail or Elise builds a fire. The flare of propane under the water kettles first burns blue and then settles into yellow. Shapes of early risers move around, testing the water left overnight in the vacuum pots. Is it hot enough for a first cup of tea?

At 6:00, though she feels reluctant to break the stillness of early morning, the bell ringer clangs her way through the camp. Without this repeated raucous ringing of the bell, the women might not wake up, and a note will inevitably appear on the pad in the communication center later, "Morning Bell Ringer, Please ring LOUDER." A few more notes appear:

> I'm thrilled to be here in this sacred place-space. Thank you to all those who created this "dream", and for working out and actively making it unfold for us at this moment in time.

> I was thinking the same during the 1st sit today—flooded with gratitude to the crone mothers for holding the space. I felt so much love—mother love—something missing from my childhood.

> Would love to have a gratitude journal we could all add our thoughts to like this.

Soon a line has formed in front of the two bathrooms in the central parking area, and the one above in Camp B. The woman at the head of the line watches and listens for the opening of the door, and walks forward to catch it as the woman coming out holds it open for her. Their eyes meet and they exchange small smiles. Like the humped gait of a caterpillar, the line grows fatter and thinner, as more women join. The loudest sound is the swoosh of the toilet as it flushes after each woman. The bell ringer clangs through a second time: the sitting will start in ten minutes. Several car doors and trunks slam shut, and there's a general movement of bodies towards the fire and the meditation area.

> I come to sitting from a 30+ year Zen practice, so I'm used to facing the wall when I sit. The 1st time I sat this retreat, the beauty in the woods was so extraordinary, it seemed unreal, and hard to fully open to it. Yet for years afterwards, the images of these woods would flash across my mind at unexpected moments. I suspected I took it in more deeply than I realized at the time.   Rhea

> I felt, looking at the trees, that my place here on earth is small and limited compared to them. Helped me keep my troubles in perspective.   Diana

Some woman-shapes are already sitting; the rest remove their shoes at the edge of the tarps, and take their places as quietly as the crinkly plastic allows. As bodies lower into sitting postures, sounds wash over us: the rub and tangle of blankets and shawls, soft coughing, creaking of canvas or aluminum chairs, a blossom of light laughter from the kitchen, a soft raven croak from above, or the sough of a wet, foggy breeze.

> The silence is really important: the agreement not to have even whispered little conversations, the freedom from social interaction.
> Connie

> I keep missing Shanti.
> Me too.
>   Gratitude Journal

> I love to watch our faces relax over the weekend as bodies sink into the precious silence we hold for one another.   Nancy H.

Even quiet sounds slowly diminish; the candle flame dances on the altar, and the early morning stillness returns. Internally, each woman experiences her own settling in: the sensations of the breath entering and leaving the body, muscles relaxing into a familiar meditation posture, a wish for loving kindness, a quiet attentiveness, a memory of an early morning dream, a feeling or thought of dread or joy or sorrow, a plan about what needs doing when she gets home. Another day of practice begins.

> I dreamed I was at a silent retreat and was rooming with two other women. They had decided that the silence did not apply to them and they were going to talk anyway. I was so angry and I tried to talk them out of it. I asked them why they came and they said they wanted to be near me. I told them to try it, that the benefits were great but they just laughed and said that they had brought novels and would read and discuss them.
>
> I went to the "authorities" to tell them about this situation but I had a terrible time finding anyone and when I did they just shook their heads and said, "You know we can't move you." I couldn't believe it but somehow knew they were going to say that.
>
> (I awoke thinking how wonderful it was that I was trying to protect the silence. Then in the walking meditation it came to me that those "Roommates" were inside of me and I had to live with that!).
>
> Elise P.

> Long periods of quiet mind. Sounds of crows, women's feet approaching the meditation space and settling in. Body interested in itself—times of feeling aligned and opened up. Felt diaphragm moving naturally. Crows calling one another and flying low over our sitting area. Bell sounded unexpectedly. Feeling of well-being, love for all the women here, and myself.   Janet

In the kitchen, Jackie and the morning cook measure out the water for the hot cereal. The igniter clicks several times before it sparks, then there's the blast of propane as it catches and burns. If it's a hard-boiled egg day, there's a soft repetitive tapping sound as the cook takes three dozen eggs out of their cardboard containers and places them carefully in an empty pot. The sound of water blasting out of the faucet, covering the eggs, startles the cook, and after carrying the heavy pot, with some help, to the stove, she hears the click of the igniter, and then the soft hiss of propane being consumed by fire.

Thank you for eggs every day. Much appreciated.
Gratitude Journal

The sky lightens, and the air is cool and still, or cold and windy, depending on the whims of the fog. Women who decided to sleep in are stretching and getting dressed, others are drinking their first cup of tea sitting at the tables, watching the tea lights flicker.

Fog, wind last night...fire sparkling... fog this morning...splat, crack, dripping on the tarp.   Rebecca

Ahh, hot water and earl gray—relief and a bit of boost to help accept the wetness.

Thank you to the angels who saved our blankets, sit pillows, etc. from the rain.   Gratitude Journal

After a while, the scent of cooking oats floats from the kitchen over to the sitting area, along with some low talking and an occasional chuckle. The activity in the kitchen increases;

the work meditation helper is setting up the serving table with fruits, nuts, yogurts, milks, and other condiments. The cook is testing the oats again, and the sound of the big wooden spoon knocking against the steel pot comes more frequently. The still-warm hard-boiled eggs lie wrapped in a clean towel in a basket on the table.

The bell in the meditation hall sounds three times. Slowly the women get up and move toward the kitchen. They bring their bowls from the tables where they left them last night, and form a line. Jackie and the cooks, smiling now, face the women. They bow to one another, to the women, and then one of them rings the little brass kitchen bell; its bright tone brings smiles to the faces of women. The cook removes the pot lids and the line moves forward, suddenly ravenous.

Soon we're all eating our silent breakfast; some women sit by the fire with their bowls and cups, others sit at the tables and look out at the sharp slant of light filtering down through

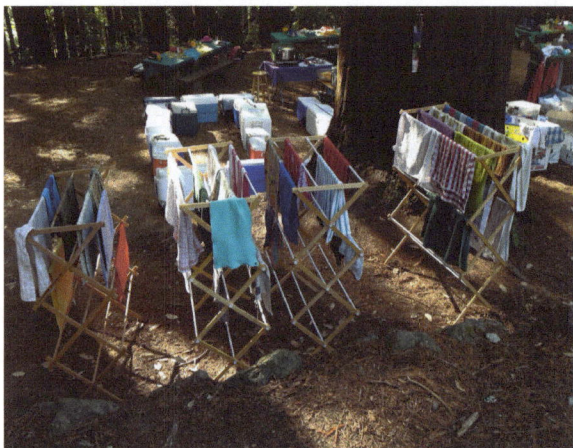

the redwoods from the rising sun. The cooks sit around the table near the stove talking quietly. The washing-up people set out the three dish-pans, one with clear water, one warm and soapy, and one warm rinse water. Women line up to wash their dishes. The food finishers put away the left-overs and hand the sticky pots to the pot washers. The second work period begins with the low voice of the cook giving instructions and the sound of vegetables being chopped for lunch.

Other women are in line for the bathrooms or are brushing teeth at the drinking fountain. Tent zippers are pulled open and shut, and the metallic slam of car trunks adds punctuation to the sounds of the morning. We hear the footfalls and voices of a few early hikers coming through the camp; and then abruptly, their voices quiet and only the sound of their boots walking on the blacktop is heard. Sometimes they stop to look at the map, or at our camp, before they continue down the mountain. The bell for the 9:00 sitting rings, and footfalls start walking toward the hall. The rest of the morning is spent in alternating periods of sitting and walking meditation.

Here's a poem by Izumi Shikibu:

> Watching the moon at dawn
> Solitary, mid-sky
> I knew myself completely
> No part left out.

I used this poem as a walking-rhythm koan this morning, but my memory said "accept" instead of "know." I think I could be content with knowing and work towards acceptance. The adventures of the mind are familiar. I recognize so many junctures, side alleys, and byways. Right now it's undifferentiated unsatisfactoryness. Moments of joy and beauty, followed immediately by aversion and dis-ease. I want this, I don't like that. What advice would I give myself? Keep walking, keep sitting. It will change.   Janet

Having a disability that greatly affects my balance, I have a difficult relationship with slow meditative walking. At first I thought there was no way I could ever do the walking, as I would just fall over. At my first retreats I opted out of it completely, substituting repetitive moves on a yoga mat, which were not really equivalent.

Then one year at Mount Tam, I decided to give it another try and found I was able to do it for short periods. The next year I moved it up to doing it most of the time except for the nighttime walk when the darkness makes it impossible for me to balance. This year I not only did the walking most of the time during the daylight hours, but I found it to be riveting and joyful. I could feel more of my foot on the ground than I ever feel in normal walking. Slow walking takes everything I've got to balance, which makes it so good for concentration; I cannot let my mind wander or I am done for. I felt at times as if I were dancing with the earth as I walked—it was a kind of one, two, three, waltz rhythm. I remember that rhythm following me into lunch where I continued to sway. The time would fly by as I pushed

my consciousness into my feet where it so seldom lives. Feet kissing the earth, dancing with its rhythms, my mind quiet.

There were two rocks at the point at which I would turn to go the other way. These rocks gave me such joy as I noticed them in the varying lights. We were in it together. Elise P.

Then it's lunchtime and we line up in the kitchen area again. Then right away, it's time to clean up, or rest, maybe take a hike. The sun moves overhead if we're lucky enough to have a sunny morning, or the fog swirls around and we feel the chill of the ocean that's held within it.

By the first sitting in the afternoon, the fog has usually burned off. The afternoon sun slants down through the denseness of the redwoods' growth, looking like shafts of sunlight through the kelp bed in the ocean just two ridges over. It's time for tea, our evening meal, then for the evening sitting and walking.

What amazing catastrophes I imagine! Do they come unbidden? I want to be prepared? Without them, I would worry less?
Rebecca

General complaint: I am in a period when even the loosest waistband is too tight. I eat without enjoyment. I don't know when I'm full. I eat past that point if I even notice it at all. I'm trying to be kind and patient with myself because I know it will change. Time to walk. NO part left out.   Janet

On a clear night when the sun has set, first Venus might appear, and then some stars are visible. The hushing of a breeze in the redwoods makes itself known, or the dead calm of the air might be palpable. When the final bell rings to end the sitting at 9:30, it's dark. The fire is dying down and someone breaks it up, the altar candle is blown out, and headlamps and flashlights show the way back to our tents. If the moon is nearly full, we can find our way to bed by its light alone.

Sunday comes with the sounds of the weekenders packing up their things, a few scattered conversations and the thud of car trunks. After lunch the women who are staying often go for a hike or find a place to sit farther away from camp while the closing circle for the weekenders takes place. As the women who are staying start their next sitting, they hear a few final bursts of laughter, then the sound of cars starting and driving up the road. Slowly the quiet returns. A pair of scrub jays starts an argument, pulling in other jays who want to share their opinions. The discussion goes on for a long time and slowly disappears into the quiet of the hot afternoon.

Afternoon sit: Nuthatch squeaking and tooting at treble and bass...junco, chickadees. Bay, poison oak, snowberry, live oak, native maple, (yellowing,) the silver green on fibrous furry redwood bark. Sun has baked the redwoods: warm air scented with wood fragrance. Gentle current shivering backbone, pressing against the skull, the closed door...at the edge. Mind skips and chatters. Rebecca

I was more acutely aware of the fragility of it all, with change just a breath away. My mom and uncle died this year. One of my cats disappeared 3 weeks ago. Shanti isn't here this year and I am watching us all age. Gratitude Journal

Chapter Four: The Silence Deepens

Attending,
The forest vibrates
Oh, so do I
    Elise P.

The Hall has been rearranged: the ones remaining have colonized the spaces left by the departed women. Preparation for tea begins during the late afternoon walking period.

The sun has fallen lower in the sky and disappears behind the ridge as we eat, clean up and sit again. By the time the bell is rung to end the last sitting, it is completely dark. A few flames lick the charcoal left from the last log burned. The sitting ends. The moon won't rise for a few hours and we stand in line to brush our teeth in the dark with only an occasional headlamp flicking on and off.

Revelation

Silent meditation begins
like fog settling in for the night
surrounding all your singularities
with shrouded fingers until
all merge into one covered
with a soothing blanket
so quiet
so pure

You've come, hungry for
judgments to crumble under
the weight of compassion
for failings to transform into
acceptance into empathy
and understanding until
your soul is
renewed
But life is never what you
imagine for how could you
foresee the monolith of your
expectations breaking open
to reveal the radiance that
exists in every single
imperfect
moment
      Kathy R.

     I love that five days are available to be silent. (I've never been on less than 5, and feel incredibly lucky that I've had that full time.) I don't know if the retreat would be possible if it were all five days for everyone, but that would be really sweet (without the disruption of people leaving Sunday.)   Connie

Still three days left. At the first sitting on Monday morning, nearly every cushion or chair in the hall is occupied. We are connected by our intention, walking gracefully around each other, holding the door to the bathroom for the next one in line, silently courteous and thoughtful of each other. We renew our intention to keep practicing. We grow quieter; we drop down deeper inside ourselves. Each woman dwells within her own body/mind. Old stories are reawakened, losses reexamined, thoughts confuse or brighten. Time slows and almost disappears. There's just the bell, calling us to sit or walk.

I found the speed of love today as I always do at this retreat. That's why I come—not to gain enlightenment, but to find happiness at the speed of love.   Elise P.

Dream: I'm sitting at the side of a road with my legs sticking out into it. A little toddler comes along who's just learning to balance and walk. He/she bumps into me and I say hello warmly. I then look up to see a woman--the mother that the child belongs to. She tells me she's off to say prayers and/or give a spiritual talk.
(The dream expresses my experience of the retreat as being a place to listen to spirit and/or prayer as we sit to regain our balance in walking gently upon the earth.)   Teresa

To whoever brought the pears — thank you. They are beautiful as well as delicious with their stems and burnished skins.
Gratitude Journal

Another delicious meal appears on the serving table then another work period, another walking period, another night to sleep or stay awake watching the moon's passage.

For all the sits except the last one today, I ditched my chair and sat on the earth leaning against a redwood tree. I got the idea when the Aboriginal character in a novel I am writing came to me during a sit and suggested I go to the ground and let a tree take my pain. When I first sat there, the bark was situated in such a way that it massaged my back just where I needed it, that pain/pleasure mixed thing that brings release. I continue to find much support from that tree and the ground.   Elise P.

Our Own Brand of Silence

Constant and inviting sounds of
Haunting foghorns in distance
Moon getting full helps keep my spirit lit.
We come together in Silence and a need for solitude
Yet our spirits scream with enthusiasm to be together
In the redwoods another year.
We don't talk yet our heart chatter is felt by everyone
And if one woman falls in despair, grief or suffering
We hold her with loud silent intention.
We hold the sacred vow of right speech and
Vocalize only at chores and mmms for food
And Ahhs of enlightened moments
Murmurs of being lost in the woods when our meandering
On trails leads us to another woman meditator.
Always pointed in the direction of Dharma Camp.
The crows, jays, turkey vultures and occasional
Red tail hawk speak for us to remind us
Of gratitude and forgiveness and compassion
No words yet plenty of
Communication.
No eye contact yet eyes with sparkling reflections
Of souls searching for peace
No conversations heard yet plenty felt
We come together in silence yet we hear each other.

      Patti.

This year the comfort of our group left me at times not wanting to be alone in my tent but enjoying being near you all more than I remember from past times. My teachers were the usual suspects: old age, sickness, death, impermanence.

Gratitude Journal

Silence is not
Absence of sound
But an unveiling
    Elise P.

Chapter 5: Thoughts Turn Towards Home

Suddenly it's Tuesday, our last full day. Our minds start thinking about what awaits us when we leave. Either we let them wander, or we redouble our intention to practice, or both. The energy around the camp shifts.

I am trying to stay in touch with myself, move when I need to, and let my eyes open when they do. Doing my best to stay in touch and connected to myself, and be kind and gentle as my body goes through its—-whatever it needs to go through. Being kind. After this last sitting, which was so difficult, I went down for a cup of tea (something I never do) and ended up sitting near the firepit watching the golden light of the setting sun melt down the tree trunk. It was beautiful and peaceful and I was, as well, sitting calm and relaxed. Eventually closed my eyes and had a very peaceful sitting holding my teacup. Go figure.
    Janet

The heat that swells in me, what is it? New energy?   Rebecca

Those who are determined to keep practicing may stay in their tents more, or take longer walks, but so do the women who are thinking about tomorrow and what comes after. There's more activity in the kitchen. Jackie is starting to pack up the boxes and the things we will no longer need. Leftovers appear on the table for lunch and tea, and the desserts that women brought that we haven't yet eaten start appearing at the end of the table--far too many sweets. The energy rises. More people gravitate to the kitchen. Jackie puts them to work. Larger rips begin to appear in the quiet.

> *My strongest recollection was the day – 4th day I think – when several of us were sitting and nodding off in the late afternoon. Suddenly there was chanting that crescendoed and was accompanied by the brass bowl. In Tibetan no less – Om Mani Padme Hom. I finally peeked – a Tibetan girl in pigtails – and around me a group of women with tears running down their faces. Then she said "see you later" and skipped off up the road. It was all revealed later that evening but for that afternoon it was one more instance of the redwood grove providing a state of wonder.*   Djuna

> *The ravens in their many vocalizations..the so near coyote with bark and wailing call so high, causing my wide smile, nose scrunching.. the bell vibrating through me, I was air.*   Rebecca

The sittings are still clothed in silence. Perhaps fewer women come to the afternoon sittings; maybe they are taking a long hike or lying out in the sun, but the evening sittings are full and quiet. Yet, there's a restlessness underneath the silence. Inevitably, even the most dedicated practitioner feels the pull of leaving. Lights in tents stay on longer after the last sitting, and the sounds of packing bleed between tents.

> *During walking meditation, I daily took my walking poles and trucked through the woods. It felt like an integration of my newer athletic self and my older meditative self. As my hiking took me by vacationers and fellow hikers, I felt like I was bringing this integrated athletic-meditative self into the world around me. I appreciated the freedom the retreat's structure gave me to find my own rhythm and path. I was trusting I was big enough to find my own way, and that it would be right for me.*   Rhea

Wednesday morning the wake-up bell ringer notices lights in most of the tents as she passes on her first round. Some tents are already dismantled and piles of belongings lie neatly stacked. Car trunks are already thudding shut. The hot water for tea has run out because so many more women are up before the first sitting. The silence in the hall during the 6:30 sitting feels slightly more fragile: there's more throat clearing, more rustling.

Still, though, the silence holds; we can hear the soft rubbing of raven wings flying over-head, a little low talking from the kitchen, and Jackie's laugh. Most of us are happy, mulling over our retreat experience, remembering those moments of deep sorrow and joy, those trea-sured insights that came so unexpectedly.

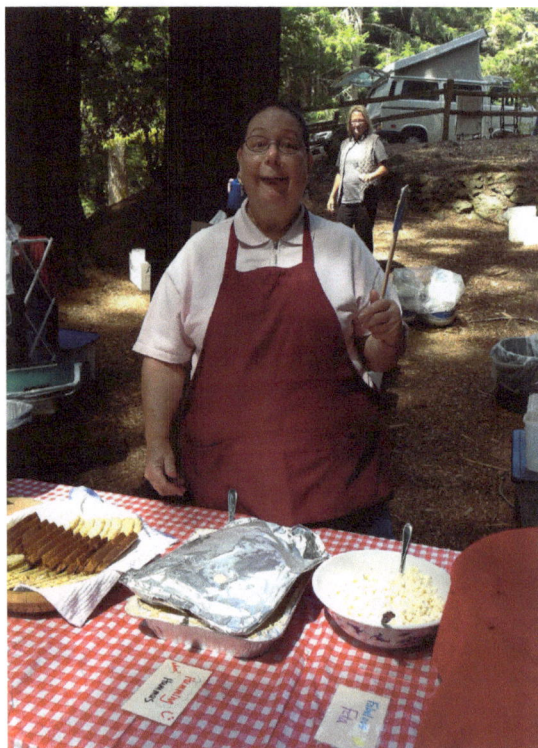

One very different thing for me is that I'm smiling at people. Instead of avoiding eye con-tact, I am seeking it out. Many of the women I've known over the years do a double take when I smile at them. What am I giving up or losing? A feeling of isolation and separateness. I feel part of the retreat as I haven't before. So many faces I know--in repose so beautiful. We are all aging, many of us have had illness, loss of loved ones, but the circle of women coming here continues. I'm not worrying about my practice. Sometimes I think, Oh, I should be doing more walking or put in more effort. But isn't my happiness evidence that I am doing it just right? Who said we could be happy and at ease on retreat? Who said we couldn't? Janet

After breakfast and the clean-up, breaking camp begins in earnest. Those women who have already taken down their tents and stored things in their cars are in the kitchen asking Jackie what needs doing. Though conversation is quiet, talking is more open now with bursts of laughter; tearing down camp requires some talking. Old friends who haven't had enough time to talk are deep in conversation. Women connect over a task and forget what they are doing. Talking is so delicious. Many voices join the Jackie chorus: Jackie, where does this go? Jackie, what do you want me to do with this? Jackie where is the box for this? Jackie how do you close this? She knows all the answers; she's cheerful and laughing. The tasks are getting done in spite of us.

Then the bell sounds for the last sitting. We stop what we're doing and make our way back to the circle. Once we accidentally left food out on the tables and during our closing circle the crows visited the kitchen, pecking right through the plastic bags, helping themselves to whatever they liked.

We gather in our accustomed places for the last sitting. There's a little more shifting and adjusting of bodies, more coughing and throat clearing, more creaking and protesting of chairs. Our bodies know this discipline is nearly over, and they are impatient to be up and moving, even as our minds long for the silence to continue. Our knees feel a little tighter, and our feet fall asleep more easily, though a few women sit still as ever.

Chapter 6: Breaking the Silence

Talkin' 'bout words
Talkin' 'bout words, feelings, sounds
That mean something to someone — to me — to you
Touch upon a clear blue sky
Focusing on what's beyond
Where it is and who we are
Can't tell you – but - you can listen
And so it works with me, too
And we share – what there is – to share
And we listen
And we speak – and even when we don't, we do
Communication ah relief
Pain, Joy, Sorrow - and all that is – beyond

Shanti

When the bell that ends the last sitting has been struck three times, and the sound has died away, Jackie invites us to form a big circle, so that we can all see one another. It takes a while for all of us to shift our things and form a circle, which has to keep expanding as people in the middle move outward. This is also a good time to take a bathroom break, because once the stories start, no one wants to leave.

When we're all sitting quietly again, Jackie invites us each to tell something about our experience on retreat, beginning by saying our first name, and maybe how many years we've been coming to the retreat. There's a moment of silence and then someone starts talking.

Feral Buddhism: A Woman Heart Sutta

No Form, No buildings,
No corners, no walls
But one flowing landscape
Moving through eating, sitting, walking,
Peeing, dishwashing, tea drinking,
Ruminating, fire watching
Unboundaried,
No separation
One flowing experience of freedom
No authority
No Buddhist standard to measure up to
No right, no wrong way to sit
Breath, practice
Radical freedom,
Feral Buddhism
Free range women, sustainably fed
Uncolonized
Undomesticated
Restored to our natural habitat
Capable
Cooperative
Independent
Collective
Trustworthy
Knowing
Connected
Sadu, Sadu, Sadu
         Betsy

When I first started going to this women's retreat I found it very empowering. To not have teachers guiding me through a retreat, and to do it by myself was a great surprising gift. The support of the other women around me there meditating in silence gave me courage to rely on my own inner wisdom and exploration. I found after my first retreat here that meditating at home by myself was much easier.   Carol H

It felt safe and ancient to be around the fire with the women. And so cared for!! Beautiful meals, a fire in the morning all ready. Such a treat for one who is mother, nurse and wife.   Diana

The stories are as individual as the women. Sometimes it's hard to hear because voices get softer when stories are so deeply personal. Often women tell about something they understood differently because of being in the silence: a relationship with a parent or child is redefined, a sickness or death accepted in a deeper way, a path forward clarified. We remember loved ones who have died or live far away. Once a woman told us that she was pregnant and that we were the first people she'd told. A woman on her first meditation retreat tells how frightened she was of the silence and that now she can't wait to tell her friends, and to come back next year. Women who have been coming since the beginning say how much this respite from their busy lives sustains them throughout the year.

I hiked miles in Muir Woods, explored all of the area near Alice Eastwood, and loved the entire experience.
When I returned home, I discovered that the bare spot on the ridge of the mountain visible from the Sierra Trail is visible from my house in El Cerrito. I understood then why I had felt such a connection to the place, as I had also come to feel with the women I had camped with.

The following two years, I had wonderfully rich meditation retreat experiences. Hiking was part of that, but the silence and community were as supportive of my practice as the formal retreats I attend at Spirit Rock. The mountain and its denizens are my inspiration for spacious awareness, the other women are my safe haven, and the founding mothers are true Bodhisattvas. In addition, it's still fun!
Nancy B-S

The year that the Summer Olympics had just concluded before the retreat, I remember saying in the closing circle that I wished the Olympics had a contest that rewarded the slowest walker. Just think if we could see the importance of slowing down, that ability to interact with the environment, with the body, noticing, noticing as we go. How important the noticing!   Elise P.

Before this current retreat, I had not sat 5 days in over a year, and had forgotten how heart opening and powerful it is to do. Sesshin (sitting meditation) almost always feels like a real home-coming for me. Being so immersed in nature, I felt it's powerful neutrality, with all the aliveness this awareness generates. Living and sitting within the bigness of these woods, the strength of women sitting so still with me helped me open my heart and surrender to the moment. The felt sense of this continues to live on in me.   Rhea

I am so grateful to have been a delighted participant for so many years--I wish it were all of the years, but the spirit of our time together bubbles alive in me even by remembering. Thank you all from the ground of my being!   Nancy H

We also tell stories of encounters with animals or different aspects of the mountain and how we have widened our understanding. There is laughter and tears. Eventually the gaps between stories grow longer, and finally we understand that everyone who wants to speak has spoken.

During the closing circle, nearly every woman expresses her gratitude, which naturally arises for this time of quiet and internal shifting and settling. Silence this deep and sustained is so rare in our busy world. The women who have never been on a silent retreat before and who were a little afraid of it, are also elated and filled with gratitude.

When the silence is reestablished, one of us talks about generosity, or Dana, in the Pali language of the Buddha's time. In a more traditional Buddhist retreat, we are offered the opportunity to practice generosity by donating money to support the teachers, and the people who have staffed the retreat: the cooks and managers, and the registration takers. On Mt. Tam, we have no teachers, and the all the work is volunteered. However, we collect Dana because the desire to give to others naturally arises out of the feeling of gratitude for being on the retreat.

When she was with us, Shanti always gave this talk. These days it is Jackie who reminds us that there is a basket on the communication center in which women can leave cash or checks. She talks a little about how we use the donations, and gives us an update on Tsering Dolma, the Tibetan nun we have sponsored for many years, to remind us how wide the web of our generosity is cast. (Please see the appendix for more about Tsering.)

Chapter 7: Closing Rituals

After the last woman in the closing circle has shared her experience, there are three rituals that complete our retreat: the Red Protection Cord, Sharing the Merit and Offering Loving-kindness.

For the first ritual, Jackie picks up the spool of red string she has beside her. She asks us to hold our hands up in front of us, shoulder-width apart. She stands and gives the end of the string to the person to her left, then begins slowly walking around the circle, placing the string between the hands of each woman in turn. When she gets back to her seat, she says: "This string we each are holding represents the circle we have created here, practicing together on the mountain. It represents the refuge of the Sangha."

She goes around the circle a second time, this time cutting the string between each woman so that each of us holds a length of red string. Now she says, "Each of us has a portion of the circle, a sign that although we are separated, we still are connected. It may also be a protection as we leave this place." Jackie holds up her wrist and shows her string from last year, pale and thin now.

She instructs us to tie three knots in our piece of string, representing the three refuges: the Buddha, the Dharma and the Sangha. Once we have tied the three knots, we then turn to one of the women next to us and ask her to tie the string on our wrist, neck, or ankle.

The second ritual, the Sharing of Merit is done by Janet, Elise or Meira. In our Buddhist tradition this ritual is conducted at the end of every retreat. It goes something like this:

May whatever good that has come of our being here together for these days of silence on Mt.Tam, benefit not only ourselves and those we love, but also may it benefit all beings everywhere.

I missed the closing ritual this year, for the first time after all these years.

I missed the unique heart thrill of looking in the clear light-filled eyes of wild women meditating in the woods.

I missed hearing the stories crafted in silence and nature of the past year told with open vulnerable hearts.

I missed the tears of joy, grief, anger and sadness.

I missed the ritual of the red string with the knots of the Buddha, Sangha, Dharma, which I always place on my right ankle.

I missed the explanations of inside jokes that had the cooks and helpers whispering and laughing with that special withholding quality only heard on retreats, that simply drove me nuts with monkey mind on at least 2 sits. Yes, always a healthy distraction from my own festering thoughts.

I missed supporting women who had losses, illnesses, and painful unwanted transitions.

I missed witnessing the joys of new life, new jobs, new relationships, adventures, travels as well as juicy beginnings.

I missed weaving new colors and patterns to the memory bank in my heart and mind for the Mt. Tamalpais Women's Retreat.

Patti

The third ritual, Metta or Loving-kindness, is a natural outgrowth of sharing the merit. There are many variations of the Metta ritual; this is the basic form:

May all of us here be happy and peaceful, may we be filled with loving-kindness, may we be safe from inner and outer harm, may we be free from suffering, may we be at peace with ourselves and one another, and

May all beings everywhere be happy and peaceful, may they be filled with loving-kindness, may they be safe from inner and outer harm, may they be free from suffering, may they be at peace with themselves and one another.

Chapter 8. Breaking Camp

Women are still packing their belongings into their cars and the thud of trunk lids is everywhere, This time, though it's accompanied by voices talking, laughing, shouting.

And somehow everything: all the pots and pans, the first aid kit, the hand lotion and tea lights, the coolers, everything that we carried in has to be divided up and taken to someone's basement or garage until next year. For a while it seems as though there is more to take out than we brought in, though, of course, that's not possible since we've eaten most of the food. Someone volunteers to take the uncooked food and leftovers to a homeless shelter. Someone else is loading bags of compostables into her van. Several women are helping Sarah pack her things back into her car, and Jackie shows others the schematic of where everything goes in her rental VW camper.

From the meditation area, women are picking up tarps and carrying them to the parking lot for sweeping. They fold them all semi-neatly into a big plastic bag and put them back into Janet's van. Someone else is taking down the prayer flags, folding them, and trying to find the plastic box for the pushpins.

Someone walks through the camp to be sure that nothing is left and finds a sign clipped to a redwood branch that's escaped collection.

It's all coming together. It's all coming apart. Cars drive back up the winding road to Panoramic Highway. The parking lot is empty. The ground bears only footprints, all that's left to show we've been here another year.

The resident crows fly down to search around the tables for anything we might have left behind. One finds a bright gold cherry tomato that had rolled under one of the tables. She pecks it, how ripe and sweet! Crow gratitude.

CLIMBING SHANTI

Moving out of Silence

Leaving for a while the forty women
sitting in silence on Mount Tamalpais,
we walked most of the way down,
Shanti and I, single file,
the four o'clock light
dripping down the trunks
of the redwoods.

We've been teaching ourselves---
feet on duff and
soft breath mixing with morning fog,
the trees, the night sky,
the ravens and the scrub jays
raccoons, yellow jackets, spiders---
how every living being on the mountain
sits and walks in harmony.

At the fork, we take
the smaller path
and climb up the creek bed,
a series of shallow pools
connected by trickling water.
At the last one, we take off our clothes
and dunk our bodies
into the cold.

It's like bathing in seltzer
after all our dust baths.
Hair sticking straight up
we laugh out loud.
A jay answers.

Short cut

Emboldened by the silence of three days
and the dunk in the cold stream
we are reluctant to go dutifully
back the way we came.

Let's go further up.
Here's a path. Maybe we can hike up
to the road and come back around
that way.

So familiar,
wanting to get off the marked trail
wanting to set out across country.
The scrub jay, urging caution, is ignored.

Let's just climb for twenty minutes
then if we can't find the road,
we'll come back down.

Even at the beginning, the slope is very steep.
The ground rotten under our feet,
falling away as we move across it.
With the slightest pressure, rocks
break away from their outcrops,
solid-looking roots come off in our hands.

Even before twenty minutes
it's obvious
the only way back down
is by falling.

We move like spiders

We move like spiders on a trembling web
of root, loose soil, decaying trees, and dry
moss brittle like dried sponges.

I think that's the road up there,
doesn't it look like a clearing?
That must be the cut.
When we reach it, it's only a path
of sunlight through the trees.

The sun is climbing out
of the steep ravine too,
keeping pace with us
on our slow ascent
up the canyon wall.

Climbing into the light

My right foot stands firmly on a broken root;
the left long since having given up on finding
anything solid.
I lie standing up against the steep side
of the canyon,
my hands range one way, then the other,
searching.
I no longer look up
I don't hope to see the road.
I don't look down either,
nor imagine myself lying
crumpled and broken at the bottom.
There is no rescue here.
Shanti, a little above me, has found
a small oak tree
no bigger than a banister.
Slowly she lowers herself down toward me
until only
her right hand clasps the trunk.
Climb up my body,
she says.

How can I do this?

My left hand reaches—not far enough.
Somehow she lowers her foot
another two inches and
I grab hard rubber, leather, shoelace.
Pushing off the last firm place I know,
my right hand finds her ankle,
grasps the rough, warm hide
of her boot. My body arches and

as my left foot finds a fleeting firmness,
right hand finds her knee:
moist and soft, it gives a little under
my fingers and then springs back. Flesh.
As dry soil falls away
my left hand finds her shoulder, and my right
grips the tree she's still holding.
Grasping her arm, I pull her up.

We both cling to the small oak tree
like the forest creatures
we've become.
The mountain supports us.
Our hands and feet are our teachers
as we continue climbing
into the light.

    Janet

Appendix: Dana (Generosity)

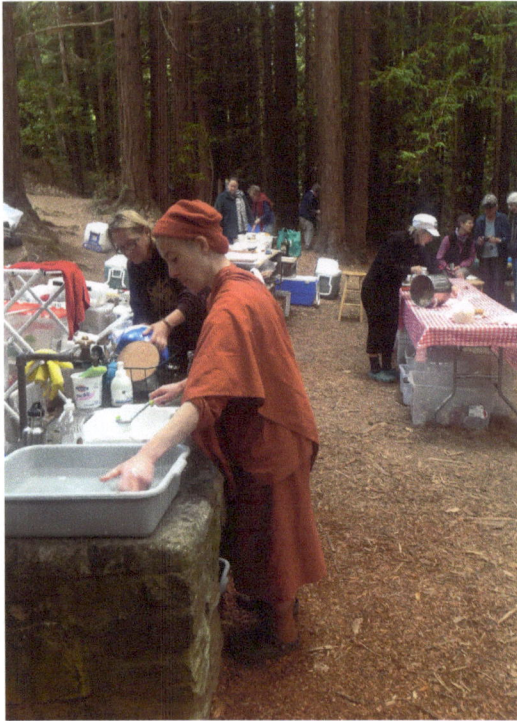

Since the purpose of our retreat is to support women in their meditation practice, we want to use the Dana donated by the women in a similar way. We allot some of it to scholarships for women to attend our retreat. In addition, we want to support women who have dedicated their lives to the Dharma. We asked for advice from some of our women teachers and they suggested donating to organizations they work with that support refugee nuns from Tibet, and nuns in Myanmar (Burma.)

For the past several years we have also donated to the Saranaloka Foundation, an organization supporting the establishment of a vihara (monastery) for Therevada nuns in San Francisco. Two of the nuns from Saranaloka have attended our retreats.

From our early days we have supported the Tibetan Nuns Project, founded to educate and spiritually support women who had escaped Tibet for religious freedom. Tsering Dolma was the first nun we sponsored. Here are excerpts from her biography:

I was born in 1976 in the Molha district of Eastern Tibet. Both of my parents are living, as well as two brothers and a sister. My elder brother is married and has two children; my younger brother is home helping our parents; my sister was very young when I left, and my parents have sent her to school.

We are samadrok, nomads who own farmland and domestic animals. My mother and sister-in-law work the fields and my father stays with the animals on pasture-land. We produce wheat, barley, peas, turnips and potatoes for our own use.

I have never been to school; my parents are illiterate so I didn't get an opportunity to learn the alphabet from them, as some of my friends did. To practice religion and to study, I offered my hair to Tenzin Thinley Rinpoche of Detsa Gompa. I did not tell my parents. I left quietly while I was with my father at our drok in the pastures. I stayed with Rinpoche at his monastery. My father came with food supplies for me, but he did not say anything. Later my mother said I did the right thing.

I stayed at the Monastery for three months; there I learned Tibetan reading and writing, but most of the time I was memorizing prayers. Our Rinpoche suggested we all go to India to learn more. My parents gave me money for the journey. Our first guide was inexperienced and we wasted many days getting lost. We had quite a difficult time with the border police; they arrested us several times and many times we ran. At one place in Nepal, we had a fight with the police; they wanted to take us back to Tibet. We threw whatever we could get to defend ourselves and they threw stones back. After a while they started firing. In the scuffle, one monk was killed and we had to hide for three days. We were so hungry after the third day that we had to come out. The police captured us, and took us to Kathmandu, where we were locked up for five days. Then a man from the Reception Center came to release us. We stayed at the Center for a month, waiting for other people in our group, who finally came. Then we all moved to Dharamsala.

When we first tried to get into Dolma Ling Nunnery, there were no vacancies. Seven of us studied there as day scholars for three years, staying in a rented house nearby. Now we are all at Dolma Ling. It is a great opportunity so I am studying hard to make use of my time here.

Each year after the retreat, Jackie sent our support to the Tibetan Nuns Project and received thank you letters from Tsering for our Dana. Gradually, a rich correspondence developed between the two women. Here are passages from the letters between Jackie and Tsering:

My dear Jacquelyn, Tashi Delek. (a Tibetan greeting which roughly means blessings and good luck) How are you? I hope you are fine and glad in your place. About myself I am fine and happy in Dolmaling nunnery. I am studying hard. I am learning to speak English so that I can talk to you. I am very grateful for your kindness that you

are supporting my education. I feel I am very lucky to get wonderful opportunity to study with your support and love.

How are you with your wonderful friends and what do you do theseday? Here I am so fine with Dharma friends. We never waste our valuable time and study hard. Here weather began to rain. All day fell down rain, it look like rain is cat and dog. Last vacation I went to Bodh Gaya for Kalachakra. His Holiness the Dalai Lama gave fifteen-day teachings and I circumambulated around the stupas in Bodh Gaya and prayed for your long life.

In 2007, Jackie received a letter from the Tibetan Nuns Project saying that Tsering had found a paid job as foster mother taking care of young Tibetan children. "Our policy is we cut off the sponsorship once the nun leaves the nunnery or is able to support herself…" After a long pause, Jackie heard again from Tsering:

Foremost I would like to say very Tashi Delek toward you and also I hope you are in good health. Sorry for my long gap silence. Today I got a very great opportunity to meet with your friends and they give me your address. [As will become clear below, one of our retreatants, Diana, went to India and met Tsering.] Otherwise I didn't get til now. And also they told about yourself that you are very kind and love to laugh too much and always attach smile on your beautiful around face. Really your two friends are very nice in everyfield and we, the home students and also included me, enjoy too much with them… Oh, also in these year my father and younger sister will be come to India. Here I am little bit problem on money on them and I promise to them before to spent money for coming in India. Please what way to understand my problem and help me. I am sorry to say on this… I am very happy with my children and also they respect on me a lot. I will spent you a letter on the hand of your friend…missing you a lot.

From Jackie:

Hello from foggy San Francisco. I got your letter and I am glad to hear that you and the children you care for are all doing well…

We are also getting ready for our annual camping meditation retreat. August

24th to the 29th I will be joined by 60 women who will be sitting in meditation outside under the spreading redwood trees on sacred Mt. Tamalpais. The women have such dedicated practices; many of them have been coming every year for 14 years…

For me personally this has been an eventful time. I am working with women who are struggling with mental illnesses and I have started an intensive treatment program to help them. It is very exciting and I am pleased to announce that we are celebrating our first year in business and we are still moving along.

I think of you often and am so proud to be supporting your good work there in Dolma Ling. [At first we didn't understand that Tsering's new job was not associated with Dolma Ling, and was, in fact, in a very different part of India.]

You are an inspiration for your selfless efforts to help relieve the suffering of those children. Sometimes I feel that the children are the ones who are touched the deepest by the sorrows of the world. And yet they are the ones who also can be helped to be strong and move on to lead better lives. When I look at the pictures you have sent of your home school I am always struck by how happy the children look. I know it hasn't been an easy life for them, and yet I see such hope in their eyes. I know that is in large part because of your love and caring for them.

Well, I just wanted to say hello and apologize for not being better about writing to you and seeing how you are doing. I will send you some pictures of our group after we meet on the mountain. Hope all is peaceful there and that you are all healthy and safe.

The next letters from Tsering were typed and seem to have been written by someone who helped her tell her story more clearly.

Dear Jackie Holmes, Thank you so much for your beautiful letter with pictures of your friends at the meditation center.

I want to write something about my present situation and about the school I am working presently as a foster mother. Our school children are those who came from Tibet like me and deprived of all those basic needs and education when they are in Tibet. So they are the one who always need my help and love.

Regarding myself, when I was at Dolma Ling I was doing well in all those religious duties as a nun. But being a poor family from Tibet, I was facing financial crisis often and my family in Tibet are also facing so many problems alike. Specially my younger sister who is in Tibet is suffering a lot in terms of everyday life and I was so much worried about her future. Being the eldest child of my family this anxiety haunts my life here and staying at nunnery would be no source of any financial support to provide them and therefore I decided to do a small job which I could earn a little and do something for them. This I promised to my parents that I will take her to India and give her modern education to make her life easier. So my father is coming this year to India to drop her also and to meet us.

As this is one of my lifetime achievement or awaited desire, to fulfill this dream I was compelled to leave Dolmaling and joined this school with the thought that I could spend a little expenditure of their journey with the amount that I earned. But the salary that I am getting at the moment is equivalent to US$50 per month which is hardly sufficient to meet the daily needs as it finishes when my small children at home asks for some penny to buy stationeries and small needed things.

I hope you will not think bad of me from coming out from nunnery. I myself feel that the real practice of Buddhism is happening here working with the small children by giving them the love and care they need and helping them at this needed stage. Though I am out of nunnery, I am doing everything according to the norms of the nun and keeping up to my religious duties. So, please don't worry.

Lastly I will ...be highly grateful if you could give me a little financial support this year to accomplish my dream of inviting my family to India. Maybe this year would be their first and last year to visit His Holiness and as I have only you to share my sorrows, hope you will give me your support and encouragement in following my dreams.

Thank you so much for your readiness to give help for my needy children.

Hello! Greetings from the Women's Meditation retreat!

I hope this letter finds you well and happy. The retreat is over for another year but it was a great 5 days in the woods, sharing our practice with each other and with Mother Nature. We had 60 women this year.

This year at our closing circle, one of the participants, Diana, shared with us her trip to India. She showed us pictures of you and the children that you are caring for at the school/home you operate. They are so sweet and innocent. We were so happy to see all the smiling faces. Diana talked about the suffering of these children and also how happy they were to be with you. We are very proud that you are doing well.

I got your letter about your family coming to visit. I hope you had a nice visit. We will continue to support the Tibetan's Nun Project and hopefully your school as well. This is right livelihood as is spoken about in the eight-fold path. I bet you are a great housemother and teacher. I also know that these children have suffered a lot in their young years. If we can help in some way, please let us know.

I have enclosed some pictures of the retreat. Blessings to you!!!!

Here's Diana's account of her visit:

When I arrived at Dolma Ling Nunnery I asked to meet Tsering Dolma and was told she had graduated! But her classmates greeted me very enthusiastically and wanted to know all about the women who meditate outdoors on the mountain.

Tsering is a house parent for these kids, all of whom are living away from their parents. In some instances the parents are imprisoned or missing within their homeland of Tibet because of their opposition to the Chinese rule. Other times parents voluntarily send their children to India to one of the Children's Villages so that they can continue to be raised as Tibetans, since they are forbidden to speak

their native language in school, have images of the Dalai Lama or practice their religion.

The conditions at the school were simple, to say the least (the kids brush their teeth outdoors.)

They are a very cheerful bunch. Laughing a lot and truly happy. I felt this was true at the nunnery too and a real lesson to me, as all the young women were refugees, had to leave their homes and families and in some cases the families would be punished by the Chinese authorities if they had any contact! Yet they were content because they had each other and their religion. This was a real "learning" for me and a shock, too, when I returned home to catch up with family and friends and listened to what sounded to me like minor complaints by comparison.

We were greeted like family there with hugs and smiles all around!   Diana

From Tsering again:

Dear Jackie Holmes, I am touched by your understanding towards my problem and attitude towards life. I also appreciate the way you had helped the disabled children and guiding people when they are in problem. We are created by the god to serve mankind. This is the greatest reward of life. I am happy to inform you that my father has arrived from Tibet with my younger sister. I borrowed some money from my friends and took them to different monasteries in South India and then to Kalachakra at Amaravathi. It was a great blessing moment and they were many people from different parts of the world to receive his [holiness'] blessings and teachings. I felt myself lucky to get Kalachakra blessings to my father. At that time, my younger sister was in Nepal Reception Center and she didn't get the Kalachakra teachings. Now she arrived at Suja and is with me. I am planning to send my father back to Tibet and will keep my younger sister here so that I could find ways to give her modern education so as to make her life easier.

I assure you that your donation in this school will never go waste. At the same time I also thank you for helping and supporting me to support my family. Your encouragement has lessened my burden and tribulations. I'll never forget you and you are my sister sent by god to look after me and to understand my problems. Hope our relation will strengthen ever more stronger year by year. Your sister, Tsering.

The next letter was written in a different hand, presumably Tensang's, whom she mentioned at the end.

I am very pleased to receive your letter and extremely happy to know about your well being and planning for the next retreat gathering. I wish you a peaceful and spiritual retreat which will bring meaning to your life ahead. I really would like to extend my heartfelt thanks to you for sending me money. I am very touched by your undying concern and care towards me as a sister. My younger sister is in the school and as she has never been to the school in her life, it is very difficult for her to study and recognize the basic alphabet and other languages. I hope as the time goes she would adapt to the learning environment of the school. I was very happy with your kind financial help I was able to repay the debt, otherwise it was a burden for me. So in this way I have not misused your money. I am further more delighted that you have ensured me that you are always there for me and this is the nicest words I have ever heard in my life since I depart from my family.

Your donation to TCV [the school] is a great noble gesture as this institutions makes life of thousands needy children and it rightly serves your purpose.

Dear Friend Jackie, Thank you so much for your beautiful letter with a lot of pictures on the retreat at Mt. Tamalpais. It's really very touching to see all the old people and the retreat sites. They brought tremendous peace and solace in my heart. ..My younger sister is at Patlikul four hours distance from me. She is doing tailoring study, learning to sew and make clothes, developing some small skills to support her life as she cannot study and go in academic line. She also get chance to learn some basic language of Tibetan and English there. Thank you for your concern towards us and my children at home in the school. Tsering

Acknowledgements

Deep gratitude to the many women who have offered their poems, journals, reflections, photographs, and art work for inclusion in this book. Like the retreat, which could not happen without each woman who comes, so too this book would not be complete without the voices and visions of each of you. Thank you.

For Writing:

Nancy Benson-Smith
Patti Boucher
Diana Corbin
Carol Hayden
Nancy Henderson
Jackie Holmes
Teresa Holtgraves
Rhea Loudon
Connie Mery
Rebecca Mills
Djuna Odegard
Elise Peeples
Paddy Rose Poupeney
Kathy Reuve
Betsy Rose
Shanti Soule (with permission of her sisters, Bonnie Karlsen and Patrice Stone)

For Art Work:

Nancy Benson-Smith, photos
Linda Bennet-Gauthier, mosaic
Patti Boucher, mandalas, photos
Diana Corbin, photos
Elise Gootherts, photos
Carol Hayden, photos
Rebecca Mills, watercolors
Elise Peeples, photos
Jane Tierney, photos

(I regret that due to technical limitations, the art works are not attributed individually.)

Special thanks to Elise Peeples, who has been a supportive ear and an invaluable collaborator in the transformation of a manuscript into a book; to Verna Lim for her technical help; and to my partner, Dave Hubbell, who has supported my practice over the years and who lent his careful eye to the manuscript.

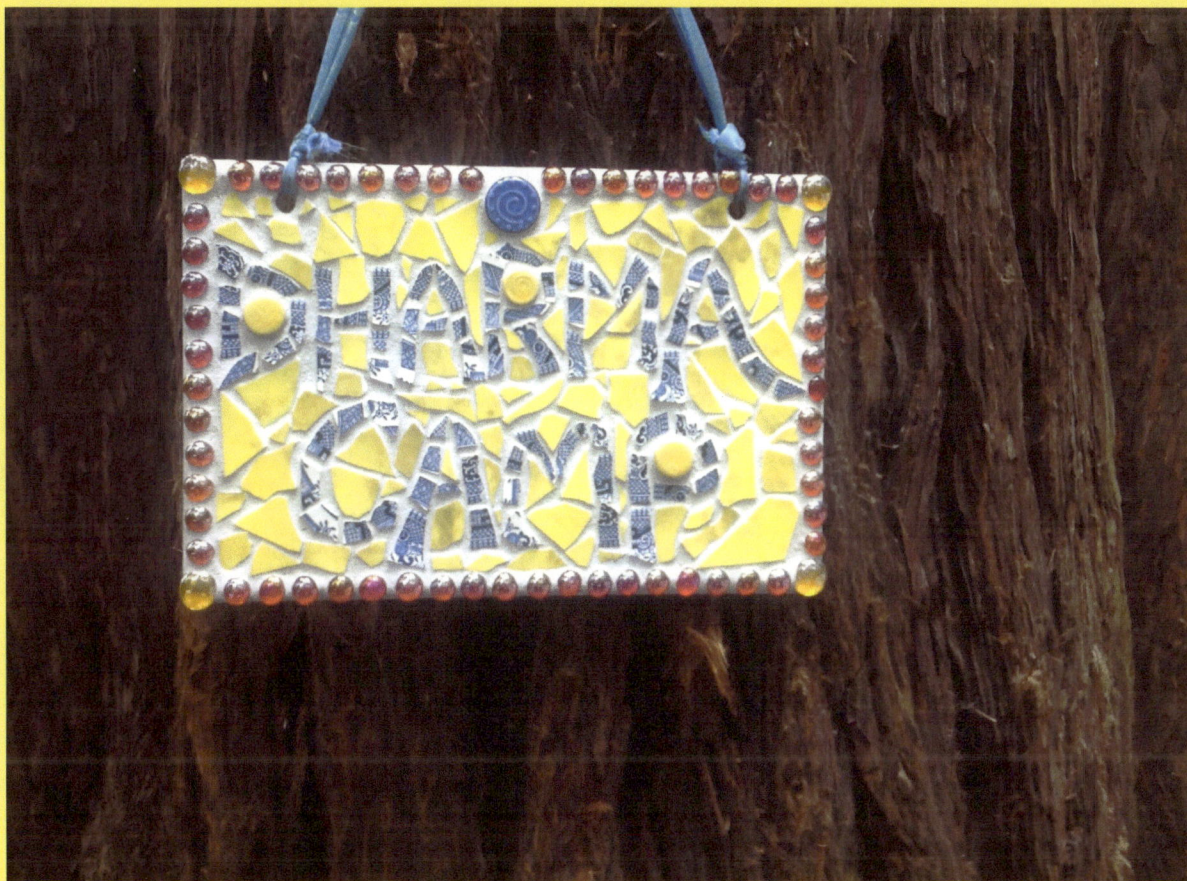

www.ingramcontent.com/pod-product-compliance
Lightning Source LLC
Chambersburg PA
CBHW042013080426
42734CB00003B/62